W9-BND-238

In Step with Jesus

In
Step
with
Jesus

Sermons by Norman Paullin

Judson Press, Valley Forge

IN STEP WITH JESUS

Copyright © 1970
Judson Press
Valley Forge, Pa. 19481

All rights in this book are reserved. No part of
the text may be reproduced in any manner without
permission in writing from the publisher, except
in case of brief quotations included in a review
of the book in a magazine or newspaper.

International Standard Book No. 0-8170-0507-2
Library of Congress Catalog Card No. 70-131421

Printed in the U.S.A.

Foreword

How many times Norman Paullin preached in his lifetime is anyone's guess. Had he himself counted — as he didn't — the answer easily might have been ten thousand. In city and rural churches of many denominations, in schools, in camp meetings and conferences, as well as in radio preaching, Dr. Paullin enjoyed a loyal listenership across several generations. His personal charisma, which was nothing less than a trust from God, developed a unique following of friends and supporters. Wherever he went, people were blessed by his spiritual benefaction on their lives and his empathic identification with their daily concerns. People saw in his preaching not so much specific principles of homiletical excellence as a forthright, simple challenge of Scripture teaching to life as it is and to life as it might become by the Spirit of God. Supported by abundant illustrations from his own experience and delivered with leisurely spontaneity and warmth, his sermons became a kind of conversational exhortation-to-remember.

Here, then, are but a very few of Norman Paullin's sermons. Absent are the intonations of his voice, gone a particular gleam in the eye and the crinkle of a smile. But preserved, because given of God in a life of prayer and Bible study, are some of the convictions he sought to share for the saving of sinners and the strengthening of saints.

HELGA B. HENRY

Biographical Sketch

Scattered here and there in Norman Paullin's sermons are homespun references to his life. These, together with items shared by his wife and co-worker, Mildred Paullin, reveal some of his experiences as a boy, his struggles as a young man, his indefatigable ministry as evangelist, preacher, pastor, teacher, and Christian leader.

The eldest of three children, Norman W. Paullin was born September 14, 1906, in the small community of Bridgeton, New Jersey, where he spent his earliest years. Later at Millville (New Jersey) High School, from which he graduated in 1924, he distinguished himself as captain of the debating team, revealing already an aptitude for public speaking. During the same period, when he was seventeen, he acknowledged Jesus Christ as Savior at Seaside Baptist Church, Palermo, New Jersey. There Mrs. Corson, a Sunday school teacher, one day after years of faithful Bible instruction challenged the young man to make the decision. Norman Paullin was but one of four or five of her boys, a class called "Buds of Promise," who eventually entered the ministry, boys who in later years were to reverence their dedicated teacher as honorary pallbearers at her funeral.

In those days the Paullin house was neither a Christian home nor one particularly interested in higher education. Lack of money was another problem. But Norman Paullin prayed and witnessed and trusted God to meet each of these needs. God, in fact, used the boy himself to bring both sisters and his parents to Christ.

The matter of further education obviously was up to him; so like many another young person he set out for the big city to find work. Making his home in New Jersey with an aunt who resented his "religious singing," young Paullin commuted to Philadelphia and plodded along almost two years in a job with the Great A&P Tea Company. Each week's personal bookkeeping compounded his discouragement. Finally one day, having again barely balanced expenditures against earnings, he confided his problems to a friend. Now this friend had just heard and been deeply impressed by Dr. Austen K. de Blois, president of Eastern Baptist Theological Seminary. With nothing to lose except a bit of his time and carfare but perhaps a whole glorious future to gain, Norman Paullin soon found himself keeping an appointment with President de Blois. "He was everything," says the report of this interview, "that my friend had said."

Having answered questions about his personal experience of Jesus Christ and having admitted to meager savings of only fifty dollars, Norman Paullin quickly voiced also his determination and willingness to work for whatever else was required. The president's reply gave not only needed encouragement for the immediate years that followed, but also a wellspring of assurance for the lifetime of ministry that was to come. "Son," he said, "if you continue to trust the Lord, you can make it. Complete this application." From then on Norman Paullin washed windows, scrubbed floors, accepted whatever work opportunities he could, putting hands and feet to his desire for further training for Christian service. By the time he left seminary in 1929, he had been ordained (July 31, 1928, at the Second Cape May Baptist Church, Palermo, New Jersey) and had served Union Church, Seaside Heights, New Jersey, as student pastor (1928–1929).

At Geiger Memorial Church, Philadelphia, his first pastorate after graduation (1929–1937), he met Mildred Strouse. Her brother, initially attracted by the sound of singing coming from the church, had subsequently been won over by challenging youth activities. When the warm, outgoing minister spoke to other children in the boy's recently bereaved family, Paullin received only rather desultory response from Mildred. She agreed, however, to join a group going from the church to attend the Billy Sunday meetings at Baptist Temple, Philadelphia. Moved by what she heard that first night, she returned alone the next evening and responded to the gospel invitation. Norman Paullin baptized her. She hardly thought at the time that she would become his wife, as she did on September 17, 1932, or that the two of them would some day have a significant ministry at Baptist Temple, where she had accepted Christ. In addition to that ministry at Baptist Temple (1948–1954), other pastoral charges, all in New Jersey, included Rosedale Baptist Church, Camden (1937–1941); First Baptist Church, Jersey City (1941–1945); and First Baptist Church, Asbury Park (1945–1948). Throughout the years, the Paullin children, Barbara (b. 1934) and Lloyd (b. 1944), entered with love and loyalty into the life and ministry of their parents.

In 1941, American Theological Seminary conferred on Norman Paullin the degree of Doctor of Divinity. Temple University bestowed similar recognition at its June commencement in 1953.

In 1951 Dr. Paullin became Instructor in Homiletics at Eastern Baptist Theological Seminary, and in 1954, Professor of Homiletics. From 1959 until his death in 1968 he served as Professor of Evangelism and Pastoral Ministry. He taught also at Baptist Institute, Bryn Mawr, Pennsylvania (now Ellen Cushing Junior College), 1954–1959 and had been on the staff of the Seminary Evening School of the Philadelphia Central YMCA (1937–1943).

In addition to teaching, he participated in the work of many committees and boards in the life of Eastern and the community and supervised the seminary-sponsored Bible study tours to the Holy Land. For the United States Armed Forces he conducted ten preaching missions in the United States, Great Britain, and France. Organizations such as Christian Endeavor, as well as Baptist youth groups, relied heavily on his inspirational leadership. A winsome and beloved speaker and leader, Norman Paullin filled responsible ministerial and denominational posts at local, state, and national levels; in 1957–1958 he was first vice-president of the American Baptist Convention.

The momentum of many years' weekly, even daily, teaching, preaching, and organizational responsibilities inevitably took its toll. But Norman Paullin refused to retire, even to lessen the work load. Motivated by his love for Christ and an overriding compulsion to preach the gospel, he maintained an almost reckless schedule. Buying up time, as it were, had special significance for Dr. Paullin, something not generally known until his fiftieth birthday in 1956. Granted a request to say a few words in chapel that September 14, he revealed the fact that none of his male forebears had lived beyond the age of fifty. Having now reached that point in his own life-span, he felt that any additional days, let alone years, would be borrowed time. As it was, God entrusted him with eleven further full years of fruitful ministry among thousands of both new and long-devoted friends.

Norman Paullin died May 27, 1968, at age sixty-one; he had literally worn out his heart in work for Christ and the kingdom. A memorial service May 31 at Baptist Temple gathered together not only seminary and other professional colleagues and friends, but also scores of men and women and young people to whom he had been spiritual father and counselor, comrade, and friend. Participants in the service included President of Eastern Seminary, Dr. J. Lester Harnish; also Dr. Carl H. Morgan, a classmate of 1929, and Dr. Albert G. Williams, class of 1930, both now retired, who together with Dr. Paullin built eighty years of teaching and of their very lives into the structure, witness, and ministry of Eastern. Dr. Walter Bruce Davis, then Dean of the Seminary as well as Professor of Missions and at that time also interim pastor of Baptist Temple, spoke on "Compelled to Do So." Gratitude for God's mercy in his own life and a firm conviction of man's eternal lostness apart from saving grace in Christ Jesus constrained Norman W. Paullin to spend himself and to be spent in proclamation of the good news.

HELGA B. HENRY

Contents

In Step with Jesus

1

Jesus Is Passing By

Jesus had but one purpose while on earth, and he has but one purpose today: to call men out of darkness into light, out of sin into righteousness, out of bondage into freedom. While he passes by, there are some who accept him and receive heaven's greatest blessing. But there are others who by rejecting him lose life's greatest opportunity.

How many arguments people offer, how many objections they raise to accepting Jesus! The One who came to reveal a loving heavenly Father is criticized and misunderstood. This Christ is bedeviled by people who want neither to be blessed themselves nor to have others blessed. Read the eighth chapter of John's Gospel. At every turn people stopped to ask Jesus by what authority he wrought miracles, from what school of learning he derived his wisdom, what great city had instilled in him his social awareness.

It became inevitable that Jesus Christ must leave untouched, unblessed, and unsaved great segments of the population of his day. He passed them by. The "them" refers to the Pharisees, religious people of that day and generation who spent time — precious time — talking about secondary things while multitudes lived and died in darkness. These Pharisees were blind and did not know it. They were in desperate need and had not sensed it. They were lost and could not believe it. But Jesus found a man blind who knew it, a lost man who sought help, a man in desperate need who did what Jesus asked him to do. Some people were passed by, some were passed up. But some, thank God, met the Savior. Today, no less than then, Jesus is looking for needy people, for men and women with needs. Jesus is passing by and he's looking for people with needs.

"We have Abraham for our father," said the Pharisees. In other words, *the* religion. We have books. We have education and social position and standing. We have everything. But here was also a man blind — helpless, dependent, socially ostracized, intellectually handicapped. Yet this man who could not see Jesus was seen by the Lord. This is the marvel: not that we loved him, but he first loved us.

I'm reminded again of the prodigal son. As long as he yearned for adventure and was driven to grasp and to get, God could not help him. But when the prodigal came to himself, saw his desperate need, and remembered the things that waited for him in his father's house, he came. God can't help anyone today who doesn't want to be helped. But Jesus is always looking for people with needs, for people with right desires.

Only one thing really matters, according to the Bible, and that is, where are you today and where will you be when the end comes? The Pharisees tried to discredit Jesus because he came from despised Nazareth. And he had no university training, they said. So-called advantages, my friends, only increase one's responsibility; for to him who hath been given much, of him shall much be required.

The Pharisees looked on external things, but the blind man desired a better state. He wasn't satisfied with himself, groping in the dark, dependent upon people, living in the muck and the mire. He wanted to be somebody. He must have had a yearning not yet satisfied, not yet realized. And Jesus was looking for people just like that. Even today he looks for people like that — people with needs and right desires.

I daresay, my friends, we're going to have the surprise of our lives when we get to heaven. We're going to be surprised at some of the absentees, and we're going to be surprised at some who are in heaven who we were sure would never get there. Let me tell you this — the greatest surprise of all will be to find ourselves there! Let's begin facing up to some things: Jesus is passing by and he's looking for men and women who aren't ashamed of their needs. He's looking for those who desire cleansing from sin, who admit their need of Christ.

While he passes by, Jesus is looking for men who recognize the opportunity to be saved. Jesus isn't fooling around. Many people think they can get right with God any time they like, they can begin to live a consecrated life when they're good and ready. All the while Jesus is passing by.

The Pharisees had the opportunity of a lifetime, but in letting Jesus go by, they passed the time, the point of no return, that marks the destiny of men either for glory or for despair.

So Jesus passed by. But the blind man couldn't be stopped, couldn't be restrained from finding help for his need. Read the stories of the blind men in the Bible and you'll discover how they pushed and shouted to be seen and heard by Jesus. They didn't want him to pass them by.

My friends, now is the accepted time. Behold, now is the only time we have.

Perhaps you've heard this story. One day a man got up in a meeting and said, "I'm seventy-three years of age. I was thirteen when I was saved and I've been walking with Christ for sixty years. Let me tell you something." And then he continued: "My mother died when I was eleven, my father when I was thirteen. Then an uncle took me in, but he didn't want me, really. No one loved me. I found I was better off on my own and so I went to London. I did odd jobs and peddled papers. Sometimes when I was hungry, I'd slip alongside a basket of fruit and just snitch a little off of the top of the pile. I slept in alleys in boxes and in boxcars. Sometimes people were good to me and gave me a bed to sleep in. I got along all right, but Sunday was my hard day. Everything was closed on Sunday; I had no friends, I had no home, and nobody cared. Sunday was such an awful day I dreaded to see it come. Well, this one Sunday I was walking along a little street and passed a Primitive Methodist Church. I didn't know what it was then, of course. Anyway, people were singing and it seemed to be a nice song. I wondered who was inside the church and so I walked into the little vestibule. Just as I stepped inside a gray-haired man came up, took me by the hand and said, 'Son, I'm glad to see you. I don't recall ever having seen you in our Sunday school before, but you'll like it. We've got a class of fellows that are first-rate. And I'm going to take you down and introduce them to you.' He pulled me over close to him; he had his hand on my shoulder; he squeezed me a little bit, looked down in my face and said, 'Son, do you know God loves you?' Well, I was taken to the Sunday school class. I didn't know what was going on; I don't know what the teacher said. I kept thinking about only one thing and later when I got out on the street, I thought my heart would break. I was sure I was going to die. I had never felt like this before. I kept saying over and over, 'I don't know who the man is. I don't know where he lives. But whoever it is that loves me, I'm going to love him, I'll love him as I never loved anybody in the world!' "

Now here was a thirteen-year-old lad who seized his opportunity and for sixty years gave his best in service to Christ.

The big thing, I tell you, is to recognize that Jesus Christ is passing by. He longs to help, to heal, to lift. You can hold back, you can sit still, you can remain silent and die without a blessing, or you can rise up and follow Christ.

When Jesus called people to follow him, he didn't ask them to know great paragraphs of doctrine. He didn't ask them to recite the Apostles' Creed. He didn't ask them to know about Postmillennialism, Amillennialism, Premillennialism. This is what he simply said: "Follow me! Follow me!"

Some people follow preachers. Some follow teachers. Some follow this. Some follow that. We ought to be following Jesus. And when we follow Jesus, he will use us in service for him. Jesus looks for people with needs, with willingness to seize life's greatest opportunity. He also looks for those who will serve him, who will be mighty through and for him.

If you have a burden today, accept Jesus the bearer.

If you're restless and dissatisfied, accept the peace and fulfillment that Jesus gives. Take him with you, wherever you go; he alone gives comfort and joy.

2

The Ever-Present Question: "What Think Ye of Christ?"

Jesus many times asked his disciples, and others as well, this heart-searching and ever-present question. He phrased it in many different ways. He asked it under many changing circumstances. Most often it was stated the way we find it in Matthew 22:42: "What think ye of Christ?" It is an inescapable and ever-recurring question. Never has it been asked but that two things have happened: Some decide for Christ favorably; some oppose and reject him. I presume this will always be the case.

When the claims of Jesus Christ are stated honestly, there will be those who stop and listen with apparent concern. There will be others, however, who shrug their shoulders and pass by, irritated and annoyed. Let me ask you: "What think ye of Christ?"

I've had the joy of joining with a friend to do personal

work; together we've asked many people about their personal relationship to Jesus Christ. We discovered that strength seems to come as two people travel and work together. Is that perhaps why Jesus always sent out his disciples two by two? At any rate, temptation seems to be less of a problem when one is not alone. And the hostile attitude of those who do not care for Christ or religious things seems far less formidable when two work side by side, when both are anxiously awaiting an affirmative answer to the inevitable question, "What think ye of Christ?"

Why is this question so important? To answer it very simply: because it is an ever-present question. The non-Christian will be asking himself: "Why should I accept Jesus Christ? Why should I identify myself with him and his cause? Why should I let him rule my life?" The Christian will be asking: "What about my relationship to Jesus Christ? Am I making him glad? Do I make an impact for him? Does my life really count now, will it have meaning in the future?" We can't escape being interested in Jesus Christ, first of all because he claims to possess all power in heaven and on earth. No one in all history has ever said such a thing. He has all the power — power to lift, power to save, power to energize, to enable, to ennoble life. That is what everyone wants — power.

Since Jesus Christ has this power, why should we not be interested in his claims? Many men and women pride themselves on being atheists. Strongly opposed to faith in a personal God, they have no time even for Providence or for the laws of right and wrong. Such persons believe that we are here to live, to do whatever is prompted by the heart, but that there is no one to whom we are responsible. Interestingly enough, I have never met an atheist who was past sixty years of age. Time has a way of mellowing life. As the years pass we recognize some of the infirmities of the body, the ebbing of strength. We become less sure, less dogmatic. We begin to wonder a bit about the future. It's rather good then to hear a knock at the door and to have someone say: "If you please, sir, I know someone named Jesus who is the entrance into the life to come." "I am the door to eternal life," Jesus said.

Actually I'm not too concerned at the moment about the few or even the many atheists in America. What I am deeply concerned about are the millions of people who are indifferent to God and who by this attitude rule him out of their lives and out of his universe. These are the ones who need to consider what Jesus said about himself.

Some perhaps may ask: "What do you think was the greatest thing Jesus ever said concerning himself?" That is a difficult question to answer, but for my part nothing gives me greater joy and greater enthusiasm than Jesus' words, "I am the resurrection, and the life" (John 11:25) and "Because I live, ye shall live also" (John 14:19). No one else that I know of has ever spoken like this. Nothing has ever so spoken to my heart nor prompted so great a response as these words of Christ: "I am the resurrection, and the life." I trust Jesus Christ because of what he said about himself.

There is another reason why I accept Jesus Christ, and that is his impact upon and significance for men and women throughout the centuries. I think it is safe to say that those in the course of history who have made indelible impressions upon their day and have blessed succeeding generations have almost always been Christians. You may challenge this statement, but the burden of proof will rest with you. While I have known people who have lived without a personal faith in Jesus Christ, yet I have never known anyone who has made a lasting contribution to mankind who was not a devout follower of Jesus Christ.

Think of Daniel Webster, for example, whose influence on American life was greater than many people realize. His faith is often acclaimed publicly by quotations from his works, such as, "I believe Jesus Christ to be the Son of God." Such convictions could not help but make Webster's life noble, sublime, and purposeful.

I don't know how many times I have read Dickens' *The Tale of Two Cities*. And I don't know why I read it so often, except that it does something to me and for me; it's an ennobling story, a story of self-sacrificing love. Remember Dickens' testimony? "I commit my soul," he said, "to the mercy of God through our Lord and Savior, Jesus Christ." Don't these words remind you of the apostle Paul? — "I know whom I have believed, and am persuaded that he is able to keep that which I have committed unto him against that day" (2 Timothy 1:12).

William Gladstone was another man who bore a fine Christian testimony. The story is told that there were three portraits in his home in England; one was of the Queen, another of Gladstone's father, and the third of his mother. In one of his addresses Gladstone tells how morning after morning he would stand before these portraits. The stern picture of his father seemed to say, "Remember, son, the Gladstones." The Queen seemed to admonish, "Son, remember England." "But," says Gladstone, "just before I left the house, I always stood before the portrait of my mother. I could hear falling upon my ears, like a heavenly benediction, her words, 'Son, remember God.'"

What a heritage! No wonder Gladstone, when asked to answer the question, "What think ye of Christ?" answered forthrightly, "All that I think, all that I hope, all that I write, all that I live for is based upon the deity of Jesus Christ, God's Son, my Lord."

Many others could be cited for their testimony to Jesus

Christ. But, let me give a third reason why you should answer the question, "What think ye of Christ?" in a positive manner. You owe it to your family and you owe it to your community to be a Christian.

When God laid his hand on me in our farmhouse in southern New Jersey, I became the first Christian in our family. Sometime later my mother accepted Christ. I wish you could have been present the night my mother was baptized. I sat in the very front row; I wanted so much to watch her confess her faith publicly. But I never saw a thing, my eyes were so filled with tears. Sometime later my sisters and my father came into saving faith. It is a wonderful thing to have a Christian family. It is a great thing to have a Christian home.

It is not easy when you are young to build a Christian home. It is something new and difficult, especially if there has been no previous example. How often I said to myself, "If only as a boy, five, six, or seven, I could have heard my dad pray!" Perhaps with this foundation I would have been a better husband, I would have been a better father and better head of the house. How wonderful it is for an entire family to be Christian!

Fathers, I am asking you: "What do you think of Christ?" You would be finer fathers and better husbands if you were Christians. Your families would be better all around if you would say "Yes" to Jesus Christ.

Mothers, your contribution is lasting. How lastingly right it would be if given for Christ!

Finally, you owe it to yourself to be a Christian. Only when you say "Yes" to Jesus Christ will you know the true joy that life can bring.

You owe it to yourself. There is a great deal at stake. Without wanting to be a crape-hanger, let me remind you how near all of us are to death even while we live.

Not to carry life insurance is considered pretty foolish. Not to have a will is also very foolish and unwise.

But you may have all the life insurance in the world and have your estate in perfect order, yet be absolutely unprepared for eternity and for an abundant life here as well. You ought to be prepared to live and prepared also to die. You owe it to yourself to settle the great issue. You ought to know, and you can know the peace, the security, the comfort, and the confidence that comes from rightly answering the ever-present question, "What think ye of Christ?" Why not settle the question and be able to say, "I have accepted him who is the Way, the Truth, and the Life. My life is hid with Christ in God. I know the forgiveness of my sins. My life is richer, fuller, and finer. My testimony from now on will be for the right. Every day I live the church will be stronger, for I make a covenant to support it and its ministry. I shall live my life for God."

John 3:16 includes you, too: "For God so loved the world, that he gave his only begotten Son, that whosoever believeth in him should not perish, but have everlasting life."

Remember the promise of Scripture: "If thou shalt confess with thy mouth the Lord Jesus, and shalt believe in thine heart that God hath raised him from the dead, thou shalt be saved. For with the heart man believeth unto righteousness; and with the mouth confession is made unto salvation" (Romans 10:9-10).

"What think ye of Christ?" It is the Lord's ever-present question to you and to all mankind.

3

The Problem of Indecision

Have you ever seriously considered the problem of indecision?

In this vast and complex world there are still many people who speak only in terms of two major divisions, the east and the west. But I would remind you that there are a great many uncommitted small nations. And there are those who would glibly characterize people as either Christian or non-Christian. But I would remind you that there are throngs of people who dangle in between, people who are neither for Christ nor committed against him. These people who are uncommitted to Christ and the church are especially haunted by the problem of indecision.

In 2 Kings 5:13 we read: "And his servants came near, and spake unto him, and said, My father, if the prophet had bid thee do some great thing, wouldest thou not have done it? how much rather then, when he saith to thee, Wash, and be clean?" What a text for people of all times and ages!

Everywhere today are great masses of people who — though they should not be written off as not being good Christians because many of them are members of our churches and have already given themselves in initial faith to Christ — nonetheless weaken the cause of Christ and make the total task of the church more difficult. Why? Because neither at home nor away from home do they do anything to keep the gospel witness alive and make it thrilling to themselves or to those around them. The supreme task of Christianity, after all, is that of witnessing to the unconverted and of challenging people to step out for God.

Look at this Old Testament story of Naaman; there is something beautiful about it. Here we see Naaman, a strong, kind man, a capable, competent individual, a valorous person highly honored and greatly esteemed by his country and by his majesty, the king. But something is eating at his very life. And we see the little Jewish maiden who had been captured and brought from her homeland to serve as a slave. She is the one who says, "I would to God that my lord were in Israel, for there he would find help through the prophet of Jehovah." On her advice and because of her concern, the decision was that Naaman should appropriate this opportunity for help. Enthusiastic about the venture, the king offered to write a letter. Even in those days, you see, it was important to know the right people who could open the right doors.

So Naaman set off in his chariot. In a second chariot were placed ten talents of silver worth approximately $17,500 and in a third, six thousand pieces of gold worth almost $52,000. Such bounty ought to be adequate to show appreciation for healing and help, healing and help being costly in any generation, it would seem. But that was not all. In chariot number four were placed ten changes of raiment, complete outfits that could be readily and easily given and presented. So, with a letter from the king, seventy thousand dollars in the currency of the realm, ten changes of raiment, and a great need, Naaman started on his journey. All this, we must remember, began with a Jewish maiden's simple word: there was in Israel a man of God, she said.

Naaman made a serious mistake almost at once, however; instead of looking up the man of God who lived in the little cottage on the outskirts of the city, he went directly to the royal palace. When the chariots drove up and came to a halt, he alighted, walked up the grand staircase, and was ushered into the presence of the king. He presented his letter. This, he was sure, would open the door of help. When the king looked at Naaman, however, he grasped his robe and cried out in agony, "Who am I? Not God, surely, that I can be helpful in this? Why was this written to me? To provoke anger and eventually lead to strife between our two nations?" Here, in the presence of dire need, the king stood helpless as a baby. And Naaman was just as needy and despairing as he was before he came. He had deposited his seemingly magic letter, but the letter was of no avail. What good now was the silver in chariot number two; the gold in chariot number three, the clothing in chariot number four?

Finally Naaman started toward the little cottage of the man of God. You can imagine the cloud of dust he and his fellow charioteers raised when they drew up in front of the little house. Looking out from inside, one of the servants, greatly impressed by the entourage, called out, "My Lord, he is here! He is here!" Said the prophet of God to the servant, "Go out and say to him that he is to go to the bend in the road to the river called Jordan. He is to dip himself seven times and he will come forth clean and fresh and healed." So the servant ran out of the house to Naaman, second only to the king in the realm of Syria, and delivered to him the message. It was a simple message, but profound. Provoked in spirit, Naaman became angry. Proud and haughty, yet with leprosy eating away at his life, he stood and said, "I thought that he himself would come." After all, if you have chariot number two with silver and chariot number three with gold and chariot number four with clothing that cannot be bought in the market, then you do not want to see an associate or assistant. You want to see the boss. "I thought that he would come." And the message: "Go to the bend in the road to the river called Jordan and dip yourself seven times." What a letdown! Can't you hear him saying: "I thought he would come and speak in the name of God, by magic lift his tender hand across the places of my need and make me well and strong! In my country we have rivers that are crystal clear — Jordan is muddy and dirty!" So Naaman commanded the chariots to pull away from the house of the prophet of God and go back to Syria. Naaman still had his leprosy; all he had lost was a letter from the king.

They had not gone very far, apparently, when something very strange must have happened. I sometimes think, though the Scripture does not specifically say so and I do not want to mutilate the word of God, that the man in chariot number four did something quite unheard of. Urging his great steeds to extra speed, he came alongside chariot three, then two, and finally up to Naaman's chariot; perhaps he crowded Naaman off the road a bit. At any rate, the text says that he dropped to his knees and said, "My Lord, if he had asked that you do some hard thing, you would have done it. To build a chapel in the woods, or a monument in the heart of the city, or a school at the edge of the desert — if he had asked you to do some hard thing, you would have done it. Why not do this? Just why?" I love the way he said it. "Why not do it like this? Just wash, and be clean."

Naaman could have run a sword through this underling if he had wanted to; such behavior was unheard of. But Naaman recognized the servant's compassion and passion; he saw the love in the man's heart. So he bade the charioteers turn around and proceed to the river Jordan. Taking off his outer, expensive tunic, Naaman walked into the river and began dipping himself. Once, then twice, then three times, then four, five, then six times. Even by the sixth time nothing had happened. The ugly lesions, the hideous disease remained unchanged. My friend, if God tells you to do something seven times, nothing will happen the sixth time. So Naaman dipped himself the seventh time, and then, praise God, the white ash marks turned to a tender pink, like the pink of a newly born babe. Out in the chariots he still had $70,000 in money and ten changes of raiment; all that he lost was a letter. Now, why, you may ask, do I tell this simple story?

The answer is not difficult to give. I do so because after many years in the ministry I am convinced that the number of people who are dead set against Christ are not many. On the other hand, those who are wholly and completely in love with Christ are not all that many, either. In other words, in the great no man's land of indecision are multitudes of people who ought to be making a first-time decision, or who should be deciding for a deeper, more effective dedication to the Lord's control. The problem is, they want to come their own way, and not the Lord's way.

Some say they're waiting to come to Christ at a certain age, or at a certain time. They're going to unite with God's people in a specific fashion. "Yes, I intend to do it," they say. "I am purposing to do it, and I know exactly how I am going to do it."

But, remember, God sets the rules, and God has a specific way, just as he did for Naaman. There was a Jewish maid who brought her witness, a man of God who knew the secret, and a compassionate companion who would not give up. Some of you came to Christ because somebody bore witness and somebody in your home or some acquaintance wouldn't give you up until at long last you gave your heart to Jesus.

The Master still has a specific way for coming to him. The way is the same for rich and poor, learned and unlearned; it's the same way for the black and white, the red and the brown and the yellow. It makes not a particle of difference what language you speak or whether you live in a big or a small house. God has only one way, a beautiful, a simple way. Do you hear it? "If he had asked thee to do some great thing, thou wouldest have done it. Why don't you just wash, and be clean?" Why don't you just take Jesus Christ as your Savior and experience new life, forgiven life, full life, abundant life?

God has his preachers, God has his followers. He has given us the Bible, and Jesus his Son as the way. Why not witness to your friends? Tell them how to find Jesus the Savior. Tell them it is not a difficult thing. Be the one person to say: "Why don't you just wash and be clean?"

4

The Devil's Gospel

If you examine the third chapter of Genesis, you'll find what we might call the devil's gospel, the prevalent thinking of today, the faith by which millions live. They say, "Whatever is natural must be right. If we had a perfect environment again, we would have perfect people. It doesn't make any difference what you believe as long as you live right." Believe it or not, those three things are to be found in Genesis 3. I'd like to talk about these philosophies because millions of well-meaning people quote these ideas as if they were the gospel, just as thousands of Christians make "Cleanliness is next to godliness" some kind of inspired truth. There are Christians who actually search the Bible for this statement and practically swear it to be one of Jesus' famous sayings. In the same way millions of well-meaning people find other notions in the Scriptures.

There are those who say whatever is beautiful is natural and must therefore be right. What a heresy of our times! But, it's just this argument we find in Genesis. Because everything seemed to be so perfectly adjusted and adjustable, the woman Eve did exactly what God said she ought not to do, arguing all the time she did it that it must be right because everything seemed so good and natural. How unfortunate it is that so many people — especially young people — take their view of life from seemingly successful people who leave God out.

In talking with young men and young women about the things of Jesus Christ and the need of becoming vitally identified with the church, one often hears, "But, I'm young. I want my chance. I want an opportunity. I want to live my life and maybe when I get older, I'll think more seriously about such things." Then they'll point to this and that person in the community who have nothing to do with God or the church, but who give themselves graciously and magnanimously to every philanthropic venture in the community. Such people may advocate all kinds of ideas. There are those, for example, who approve trial marriage, something which certainly is contrary to God's law. Nevertheless, the basis of our constitutional guarantees of human rights is the Bible.

But flippant personalities and social butterflies and climbers may say, "Well, after all, whatever seems to be an inner urge of the human personality must be a God-given instinct. So enjoy it to the full." Where does such thinking take you? It takes you to the very brink of hell — this gospel is of the devil himself and is the most dangerous thing on the face of the earth. Behavioristic philosophy tells us we ought to allow our young people to pull out the stoppers of their lives and let their natural instincts just gurgle out. Nowhere do I find that kind of admonition or instruction in the Book. The Bible teaches that my personality is tainted with sin, given over to evil. I'm told the only way to happiness is to crucify those natural instincts. Then, and only then, will I be able to stand in my day and generation, not as a beast, but as a redeemed personality whose right to live and whose ongoing life is guaranteed by the precious blood of Jesus Christ.

Let me tell you: the greatest impulses you will ever feel are the impulses given you by the blessed Holy Spirit. And when you are inspired to do something by the Holy Spirit of God: Do it! Do it!

A second philosophy popular today is, "Just give us a perfect environment." Go back to Genesis. Here's the Garden of Eden and the devil walking around in it and saying, "What a beautiful place this is, but look, you haven't explored all of it yet!" That's what we keep hearing in our schools and colleges, what we read in magazines and newspapers. This idea is advocated by government. We're told to lift the whole level of society by giving to everybody, not just an equal right, but a pleasant environment. There are plenty of homes in our country without bathtubs. But, bless my soul, the presence or absence of a bathtub doesn't make you a heathen or a Christian. It's whether you have personal faith in Jesus Christ that makes the difference.

I believe in settlement houses, I believe in a change in tenement districts, and I believe in government housing; but I recognize an inherent danger in these things, too. You can get the finest kind of a government housing project established in the midst of a slum area. You can put in it people just as they are, and unless they are changed by the power of the Spirit of God, you will have a hellhole just the same. A change of address will not change human nature. A perfect environment comes as men and women find and understand the reason for it. And the reason for it lies in correcting a human nature that is contrary to the will of God. What everyone needs is a vital personal faith in Jesus Christ; when this has cleaned us up INSIDE, then we shall clean up everything OUTSIDE and make a heaven here on earth.

Although a perfect environment will not make the people living in it perfect, we do have a responsibility to follow through when our faith in Jesus Christ has cleaned us up inside. In the Gospel of John, Jesus said that we become clean through the word which he speaks to us. His word to his disciples was: "Love one another as I have loved you" (John 15:12). When this word abides in us, then we will do all that we can to make the world a better place to live. The transformation that takes place within us when we accept Christ is the beginning of a change for the better in our world. We become part of God's new creation.

There's another thing to notice in the devil's conversation with Adam and Eve. The devil says, "It makes no difference what you believe, just as long as you live all right." Have you noticed the tricky way the devil came to Eve? He asked her, "Are you sure God said that?" Then when Eve tried to justify what God had said, the devil shot back, "But he didn't mean it just like that. You're putting things into God's mouth that he never meant. Certainly you won't die." The devil is saying to Eve, as it were, "God's just kidding you. It really doesn't make any difference what you believe." Isn't it strange, my friends, how many people believe that?

I've had people say to me, "I'm very broad-minded." Do you know what they're really saying when they say that? — "I'm so broad-minded." They're actually saying, "I'm so broad-minded that I can take you in. You're narrow, but I'm so broad I can take you in." But, believe me, someone who says he is so broad is, in fact, simply saying, "I've never quite gotten in. I guess I'm still floundering around out here. I'm just broad-minded, I just don't believe much of anything."

My friends, what you believe makes all the difference between life and death. And you cannot live a life well-pleasing in God's sight if you do not believe what is right. But where will I find what I ought to believe? Will I find it in a church? Will I find it in a statement of faith, in a creed? Listen, my friend, if I've said it once, I've said it a thousand times: Whatever you need to know you will find in the Bible. This Book tells me, "All we, like sheep, have gone astray." I'm one of them. This Book tells me there is no name given among men under heaven save the name of Jesus Christ for salvation; I believe that, too. This Book says, "No man cometh to the Father but by me." I believe that. "If you confess with your mouth and believe in your heart that God hath raised Jesus Christ from the dead, thou shalt be saved." I believe that. "In my Father's house are many mansions and I go to fit one up for you." I believe that. "If I go to prepare a place for you, I will come again to redeem you unto myself that where I am, there ye may be also." I believe that. "Go ye into all the world and preach the gospel to every creature." I believe that.

I tell you, it makes a difference, a big difference what you believe. Build your faith on the trustworthiness of this eternal Book. Here you will find the truth, God's truth.

5

This One Thing

"Brethren," said the apostle Paul, "I count not myself to have apprehended, but this one thing I do" (Philippians 3:13). If you were to ask me why Paul made such a profound impression on the day in which he lived, I would say the answer is to be found in these few words: "This one thing I do." Many of us, and I fear too often even those of us who are called to give full-time service to Christ, are more properly characterized by a phrase something like "These forty things I dabble in." Paul said, "This one thing I do."

The amazing thing is that the men and women who have followed Paul's pattern of life discovered it not only did something for them personally, but also benefited the cause of Christ.

I think of William Carey, for example. When God saved

him, he so revolutionized Carey's life that, while Carey cobbled shoes, he at the same time was thinking missions. Keeping a map of the world in his shop, Carey marked in color all the places where Jesus Christ was not yet known. The marked spots of the earth became his special prayer burden, and in time Carey dedicated himself to go as a bringer of the light of the gospel to India. Carey was motivated by this one thing, one great eternal purpose.

Then there was Abraham Lincoln. If you were to ask me what in his life seemed to be the key to understanding his great contribution, I would point to a determinative event when Lincoln was a young man. Seeing a young Negro being sold on the block, Lincoln courageously made the statement, "If ever I have an opportunity, I will strike that thing a death blow." Only God knows how far this determination took him toward becoming a great man in his day. I wonder if he remembered that statement of his youth when as President he wrote out the Emancipation Proclamation freeing the slaves.

Think also of our blessed Lord Christ. He said, "For this cause came I unto this hour. Father, glorify thy name" (John 12:27-28). Coming from heaven's glory to this miserable world, God's Son kept his eyes fixed upon a cross and upon achieving salvation for all mankind. Never wavering from this one purpose, he lived and worked among us.

So it was with Paul. He was small of stature and perhaps not pleasing to look upon. And he was no orator in the tradition of his day. But he was a Christian through and through. And when he was saved, he was saved for a purpose. How I thrill to read about that great purpose in Acts 13! For, in effect, God said to Paul, "Before you were born, I purposed you to be a light to the Gentiles. You are to be an ambassador of good news, a witness of my grace and glory. You are to demonstrate my power in your feeble, weak life. You are to illustrate Christian truth; you are to be the builder of a better day."

And so, through summer's heat and winter's cold, despite the disparagement of friends and the ridicule of enemies, Paul kept at the job of unashamedly proclaiming the gospel. Even while working at his trade of making tents, Paul kept thinking of the unsaved multitudes. Impassioned to be an ambassador for Christ, Paul left everything behind and, journeying by direction of the Holy Spirit, determined to win everyone he met for the Savior.

Why would anyone leave his home and family and friends and travel to the ends of the earth? The love of God, said Paul, constrained him. He had one and only one purpose. "This one thing I do," said Paul. Not this one thing I've done, but this one thing I *do*. "This one thing I do" means moving toward a mark, reaching out to possess, forging ahead, overcoming obstacles.

To achieve this one great, eternal thing, Paul found it necessary to "forget the things that are past." As someone once told me, "No man ever got lost on a straight road."

What's more, no man ever moved very far forward by looking behind. Remember Lot's wife; moving forward in the direction of salvation and security and health, she looked back and stopped in her tracks. The greatest falls come from not looking ahead in the direction we are going. As Paul says, the secret of vital Christian life and service is to leave the past behind you and keep going forward.

Some people, of course, have more to leave behind than others. Paul himself had plenty of things to leave behind. Think of the friends he had made in Judaism, at Jerusalem and Antioch and so many other places. He left his friends behind. Think of the years of study under Gamaliel that helped to make Paul a member of the Jewish Sanhedrin. Think of the advancement that had already come to Paul.

All these things Paul put behind him in pursuing the one thing that now motivated his life. "Forgetting these things which are behind, I press on." What a glorious picture!

Let's be honest: most of us live very haphazardly. We never seem to get anywhere because we never seem to start toward anything. Having said that, I should also add that at times it might seem that the people who never try to get anywhere and consequently never do are really better off! But living like this isn't a very satisfying way to live. Setting a goal, mapping a course, planning everything to dovetail adds a special ingredient to life. Being able to check one's progress by a stated course gives impetus to further work and achievement. Paul said, "I press on toward the mark."

I've learned across the years that if you're heading for something, if you're aiming toward a goal, you won't worry about the things around you. You're just determined that even though these things may catch up with you, they shall not slay you. And while there may be obstacles in the road, you will try to go over or under or around them. Scriptures say you will learn to stand still, look up, and wait for God to remove the problem.

Notice one other thing that Paul said. In this business of concentrating on one thing, forgetting the past, pressing forward toward the goal, Paul spoke of aiming for a prize.

The prize he sought was of immeasurable worth: to be called blessed by the Lord.

6

Trust and Obey

I am greatly challenged by Jesus' plain and simple words when he preached the greatest sermon ever to be preached. One of its major points begins like this, "Therefore I say unto you, Take no thought for your life, what ye shall eat or what ye shall drink" (Matthew 6:25). The Master is saying, in other words, *"Please do not worry."* Nine tenths of our lives we spend worrying about what to eat and what to wear. Evidences of such worry line the faces of multitudes and cannot be concealed. Deeply etched in our faces, these lines have come not because we have been happy and contented, but because, for the most part, we have been anxious and under pressure.

I've asked myself again and again, "What kind of people were these to whom Jesus spoke? What kind of folk made up that first great congregation?" As I read the introduction to the message, as I listen to the conclusion and watch the people go, I discover they are very much like us. There are men and women of many years; there are boys and girls; there are eager and enthusiastic young people and couples who have already grappled with the complex problems of their time, and who long for some kind of satisfying solution.

But isn't it strange that, in an outdoor chapel with only a big stone as a pulpit, the greatest preacher ever to come from the glory land should say, *"Do not worry"*? He uses two unusual illustrations, and how beautiful they are!

"Behold [says Jesus] the fowls of the air: for they sow not, neither do they reap, nor gather into barns; yet your heavenly Father feedeth them" (Matthew 6:26). And then he continues: "Consider the lilies of the field, how they grow; they toil not, neither do they spin. And yet I say unto you, That even Solomon [the wisest man in the world and the richest, too, I guess] in all his glory was never arrayed like one of these" (Matthew 6:28 and 29). When I read these two exhortations, I wonder if the fact that we must work is what makes us worry. Does not Jesus say that the fowls of the air do not sow, they do not reap, they do not gather into barns? And the flowers of the field certainly do not spin. Do you suppose that God's cure for worry is to stop working? That, I can tell you, would suit a lot of people.

Let me add quickly, however, that a man with idle hands will soon find something to do. It isn't work that causes worry; the lack of it sometimes does. But you've missed the whole point of the illustration if you think that Jesus is talking about working for a living. Let me tell you something: The busiest little animals on the face of the earth are the fowls of the air. For one thing, it's a tough job to go out into this old world and to woo and win a mate.

Some of those birds put up a pretty stiff fight – have you ever watched them? And as soon as a bird of the opposite sex says, "Yes," the job of building a nest begins, and of raising a family, then of training that family, and sending it out into the world. Why, you've heard it said time and time again, "It's the early bird that catches the worm." I tell you, birds work – they work hard for a living and a livelihood.

So this isn't what Jesus is talking about – getting rid of work and thus of worry – not at all.

Now let's think about lilies. Have you ever pumped an old pump handle? Have you ever pulled God's water from the very bottom of the earth and watched it pour out of the neck of a pump into a bucket? Oh, not just enough to get a drink of water, mind you. When you come home from school and Mother says, as I heard it many times in the past, "Fill up all the pots and all the kettles and all the watering troughs," that's something different; that's work, let me tell you. Maybe you've seen some of the Moody Science films. One film showed plants pumping, pulling moisture up out of the soil, and sending it out through all the plant fibers into every leaf. And out of the earth, plants pump chemicals that are distributed into the stems and become part of the buds and the flowers, and eventually the fruit. Ah, plants are working day and night all the time! It isn't the lack of work.

What then is God's cure for worry? What did he mean, when in that great sermon of the long ago he said, "Take no thought for tomorrow"? He talked with groups of men and women whose minds and hearts were constantly baffled with the problems of life. He saw how men were crushed by the weight of responsibility, how women lost the charm of youth and beauty in the daily drudge and grind. Jesus recognized the pain and suffering inevitable in that kind of life and said, "Seek ye first the kingdom of God" (Matthew 6:33). That's the secret.

The Master says if we're not to give thought to the things of tomorrow, if we're not to worry about food and clothing, about our jobs and work, about our family, and about our day and generation, if we are not to worry about the present and the future, we must put every ounce of effort we have, we must focus all our powers, we must concentrate every thought upon *one great thing:* we must seek. We must seek his kingdom.

Do you know what will happen? Let's get back now to the fowls of the air and to the flowers of the field. The fowls of the air are always seeking their kingdom. Something inside that little breast, in addition to the heart of the tiniest bird, preserves that small creature from the North to the South and from the South to the North. Those that cannot stand the damp, rough climate along the ocean are brought to sheltered and secluded spots. The hardy ones rest loftily on the giant rocks and crags of the great mountains of the northwest. All of them seek to fulfill their God-given destiny. And so they woo, and win, and build, and multiply, and travel, and sing a bit, and die. But they seek their kingdom.

Now take the flowers. They really amaze me. You can put a plant inside a room, away from the light and the sun, and it won't be long before you see how all the energy of that plant — all the climb and the drive of it — has turned in the direction of God's sun and God's air and God's light. Content and satisfied and working hard at the job, it tries to fulfill its God-given destiny — to live, to grow, to blossom, to bloom, and to die. Jesus said, "Consider the lilies of the field."

Think of the sunflower, with its face open toward the light, how it feels the tremendous pull upward at noon

time, then turns its lazy head, and lifts its face in gratitude to the West at night. It's always seeking to fulfill its
God-given mission.

Do you know when the flower world would begin to
worry? Do you know when we would have chaos in the
bird world? Havoc would result if an organizer from some
labor union showed up and said to the sparrows, "Now
look — you know you're despised in lots of places. Let's
perk up and get organized and eventually we'll be peacocks.
True, we'll have to strut a lot, but I think we can make it
on six hours a day, five days a week, with double time for
overtime and plenty of vacation time in between." Friends,
when you get a sparrow wanting to be a peacock, you've
got somebody getting out of his kingdom. No wonder
Jesus looked straight at the people of his day, and down
through the years to you and me, and said this. The great
problem in so many of our lives is simply this: We have
never yet even got into the kingdom. We have never yet
sought it with all our minds and hearts. We have never
sought to fulfill our God-given destiny. Our destiny is to
become all that God has intended us to be.

God made us to be somebody. Let me say this reverently;
God made you to be somebody. You have mind and in-
tellect, sensibility and will. Why should you be less than
you ought to be? He gave you feet to stand upon and the
ability to lift up your face and to climb high. And he did
all this in order that you might have fellowship — not with
the birds of the air, nor even with the flowers of the field,
nor the beasts of the forest — but with him.

I think Augustine was right when he said, "Thou hast
made us for thyself and we are restless till we find our rest
in Thee." Seek ye FIRST — you see, there are two ways
of seeking. You can seek, like a woman seeks for a burglar
under the bed. She's afraid she will find him and she

knows she would die if she did, but she seeks. Then there are those who seek for a job, praying all the while they'll not find it. But the word "seek" is a driving word. In the original Greek it's a word used in athletics. It means straining every muscle of your body, bringing everything into subjection as you drive for a goal. That's what you've got to do if you're going to be religious. Seek ye *first* the kingdom of God.

First means giving it just that one spot in life that's preeminent and vital. Oh, how clear it is! A man who seeks to please God is not worried about what other people think or do. The man whose life is hid with Christ in God is not worried about his flesh. The person who has a mansion in the sky is not concerned about the ordinary things that constantly pull people down here. The man who has settled the great issue with God and has wrestled and come out victorious and today is named as a child of the King — that man is not concerned with lesser things. Seek ye *first* the kingdom of God.

Just as the sunflower watches the sun, just as the trailing vine pushes through to the light, just as the little bird makes its nest suitable for itself and sings its song and dies, so I, as a child of God, am to seek *my* kingdom. And *my* kingdom is fellowship with the eternal God — to walk and talk with him who holds the universe in his hands. And the promise of the One who preached to these people with needs just like yours and mine, the promise of this One was: If with singleness of purpose, you will seek *first* the kingdom God ordained for *you*, then all of these things — I like the way he says it — all these things, food, clothing, shelter, and all the rest of the things that we worry about, will be added unto you.

If then you would know God's cure for worry, stop looking at this and that and the other thing. And stop being concerned about your big ego. Get your mind and your heart off of *yourself* and keep saying, "Lord, what wilt thou have me to do?"

If you accept his answer, you'll be the busiest person on the face of the earth and the happiest. Believe me, it's worth trying!

7

Unfaltering Trust

I have often said that I consider the Book of Job to be among the most helpful books in the Bible. Why? It contains and deals with the whole range of human experience. Nothing you will ever experience, whether joy or sorrow, tragedy or rejoicing is absent from this great Old Testament book. Its words speak of discouragement and of victory, of God and of the devil, of life after death, of the true and of the false — the list is long and comprehensive. For all that, the book appeals to me especially because of its concentration on Job.

Job believed God. He was a spiritually minded man, a person who knew how to pray, a saved man in his day and generation. God himself said Job was perfect, upright, feared God, eschewed evil, was profitable and prosperous, and there was no man on earth like him.

All of us are grateful for compliments that come our way from friends and acquaintances. But, believe me, it's much more important what the Lord has to say about us. And when God says a man is good, as he did of Job, and that there is none on earth like him, then that person must be a good man indeed. But there is further proof in the Book that Job was the kind of man God really liked. You remember the story. Job's life and testimony, his power among men was such that it plainly bothered the devil. The devil wanted Job more than anyone else, and he decided to talk to God about it. Standing before the Eternal One, the devil said to God, "His faithfulness to thee is because thou art good to him. Strip him of all thou hast given and he will not only deny thee, he will curse thee to thy face." So God said to Satan, in effect, "We'll see about that." And then a battle began that involved heaven and earth, time and eternity, God and the devil, angels and men. In it all, even when his world seemed to crumble, Job nonetheless loved God with all his heart and sought to please him.

It goes without saying that many of you have undergone great affliction; some of you have had bodily pain; many of you know what it is to have gone through hell. But let me tell you, no one, and I mean no one, can match what Job went through. According to the Scripture story, everything was going well for Job when one day, out of the blue, a servant came and said, "Job, something awful has happened. The other servants and I were with the oxen and the asses when your enemies came and surrounded us. They killed everybody but me and stole a thousand oxen and five hundred she-asses. I'm all that's left to tell you."

While he was still speaking, another servant hurried in and burst out: "Job, something awful has happened. I was in the field with the other servants when suddenly a strange fire seemed to come out of heaven and bounced across the field, and burned up every one of the seven thousand sheep grazing in the pasture. What's more, all servants but me were destroyed, too."

And then another servant rushed in with his report. "Oh, Job, something awful has happened! I hardly know how to tell you. The other servants and I were attacked out of nowhere for no reason at all. Everyone was slain but me. And the camels — well, all three thousand — every last one of them is gone, too."

Believe it or not, while this servant was speaking, a fourth one came running in with tragic news.

My friends, if the devil is interested in you, he's *really* interested. If he isn't interested, he won't bother with you. It's possible to be so self-righteous, you know, and have so little spiritual vitality that we don't pose any kind of threat to the devil. But when the devil does come, believe me, he never comes at us with just one blow. Anyone can stand up under the stress and strain of one terrific blow. But not many of us can take two, three, or four.

So the fourth servant, his face white with terror, blurted out: "Job," he said, "something awful has happened. All your children — every last one of them, your three daughters and seven sons — were together in their eldest brother's home when a great wind came. It seemed to come from every direction, and all at once the house collapsed and was crushed. Every child is dead."

I've known families that lost every child. In some it was one, in others two, or three. But to lose ten! To see their bodies lowered into the earth, to watch loving hands cover them with the soil would be more perhaps than I could take. Thank God for grace — God's marvelous grace.

What about Job? Scripture says Job bowed his head, looked up, and said, "The Lord gave and the Lord has taken away. Blessed be the name of the Lord. Naked came I into the world, naked shall I go out."

Even in this situation Job did not sin. So the devil went back to God and said, "Now look. With that last blow I had Job on one knee against the ropes. I want another chance. I know what you said. You told me before I could strip Job of everything he possessed, but I was not to touch his body. But this time. . . ." So God said, "All right, try again." The Scriptures tell us then how Satan beset Job with boils — not just with two or three, bad enough as that would be, but with boils from the top of his head to the soles of his feet!

When health is gone, it's a temptation to weaken in our faith. And here was Job, covered with boils, crying out to God about this affliction he could not understand. Then came another blow. You can suffer the loss of everything you possess. You can even lose your health and still keep faith. But then came Job's wife. "Job," she said, "I just can't take it any more. What have you done? I certainly don't know where God is. Why don't you curse him and die?" When someone you love and with whom you've gone through everything suddenly feels that God has forsaken the family because of you or something you've done or not done, believe me, that's a blow that most people can't take. Even then, however, on both knees, against the ropes, Job wouldn't give up his faith. "Yea, though he slay me," said Job, "yet will I trust him. I'll die, believing God."

This wasn't the end, however. The devil always has helpers and now a group of people came from the church. Call it the Sick Committee. They brought flowers and long faces and miserable, wretched spirits. They sat down and folded their hands and said, "Job, we've been praying about you a long time. What have you done that you've never confessed? You know God never allows these things to happen to his own." Have you ever wondered why the devil didn't bother those church members? Why should he? He had them all the time! They actually work for him day and night and don't know it! They visit the hospital, sit down with a patient, and say, "I sure feel sorry for you. You know, the last person that had your disease wasn't nearly as bad as you are and he only lasted eleven hours." Know what I'm talking about? What great people they are! Well, when Job couldn't stand it any more, he just quietly turned to these so-called comforters and said, "I don't understand all this, either. I don't know what it all means. But I do know one thing: God is good and some day I'll talk to him face to face. Then I'll ask him about all this trouble and he'll explain it. That's good enough for me. I'm going on with God. I'm going on."

"Yea," said Job, "though he slay me, yet will I trust him." In all this Job sinned not, neither charged he God foolishly. "The Lord gave and the Lord hath taken away. After the worms have destroyed this body, yet in my flesh shall I see God, and I shall see him not alone for myself, but you shall see him, too." So the devil got the message.

Three lessons are in this account for us, lessons to remember always. Whatever happens in your life, God has a right to allow it. Whatever happens in your life, God has this right. If you're not a child of God, remember he gave you life and breath and opportunities for salvation and repentance. If you are a child of God, remember you are not your own, you belong to him. And whatever happens, God has a right to allow it. Job didn't understand why all these things came to him, but Job knew that God is God. With property gone, Job was back where he started. With family gone, Job remembered that only God can give life and only God can take it away. God determines how long or short life is to be.

The second great lesson is this: God has a purpose. Even though Job did not know God's purpose, he trusted God. You remember Romans 8:28: "All things work together for good." God has a purpose. All things fit perfectly into God's plan, God's purpose for our lives.

Then there's a third lesson: God rewards faithfulness. "It pays to serve Jesus," we sing. "It pays every step of the way." The hard places of life really teach us to know the grace of God. God rewards us here and now, as well as in eternity. It pays to be a Christian.

Job lived long enough to experience God's reward. Scripture tells us that in time God so blessed this man that he had more in his latter than in his former days. God doubled everything Job had lost, because he was faithful to him. Think of those original herds now doubled — two thousand oxen and a thousand she-asses, fourteen thousand sheep, six thousand camels, and all the servants. God restored, blessed, increased.

Then we read that Job and his wife decided to start another family! Imagine! In their old age they had three more daughters and seven more sons. And these last daughters, the Scripture says, were the most beautiful daughters to live in that part of the country. And these seven sons were the most manly, magnificent-looking creatures you ever saw. I've often thought to myself, "That's fine, but why didn't God give Job six daughters and fourteen sons? After all, he doubled everything else." Then the spirit of God has reminded me: "You've forgotten something. Physical lives were snuffed out, yes, but they were not destroyed; this life isn't the end." And so, indeed, in the land of fadeless day, a great patriarch and his wife will be gathered with a completely doubled family! Believe me, when God does something, he does it right.

8

Are You Ready?

Three words occur many times in the New Testament and are used by the apostle Paul on many occasions. I'm interested in these words because of their deep and abiding meaning. I have a feeling, too, that if I can share what I, myself, have felt about these words, other people will also be made glad and will be helped. The three words are: "I am ready."

For all of us there come times in life when we ought to be able to say these words. I remember talking to someone who was soon to undergo an operation. "I am ready," the man said. He said these words thoughtfully, slowly, earnestly, and with such depth of meaning that I could not help feeling he must indeed be ready. You see, if you say these words honestly, as you face any of life's greatest experiences, it means that you have thought very seriously and deliberately. For to say, "I am ready," means that you are willing and prepared to do the deed at hand. I am willing and I am ready to do — oh, how we need to hear this in our day and generation, how we need to hear this said by Christian men and women! How all of us need to come to the place again and again where we can say, "I am willing. I am prepared. I am ready. You can trust and depend on me." The Bible, thank God, records experiences like that, too. And thank God that the apostle Paul on at least three occasions uttered the words, "I am ready," for our example and instruction.

The first instance I refer to is found in Romans 1:15 and occurs just before Paul says, "I am not ashamed of the gospel." You know this well enough, that a man must be willing and prepared to say even that. Paul said: "I am ready to preach the gospel to you who are at Rome. I am ready to preach." Oh, what a day! I don't mean a special day like graduation from seminary, for example. I'll never forget, of course, when in the Fifth Baptist Church of Philadelphia I was handed a strange piece of paper with a lot of signatures on it and suddenly discovered I was a graduate! That day, on that Commencement occasion, I had represented the student body and had spoken on the subject, "Where Cross the Crowded Ways of Life." Then I stood in front of the church and had my picture taken; I was supposed to be a complete, finished product, a preacher, prepared and equipped. But, let me tell you, it didn't take long for me to be cut down to size and to discover that I was far from fully prepared. In fact, I soon found myself back in seminary for additional study. What I was really doing, I suppose, was taking back to the professors some of the problems I had discovered on the field that I could not answer. Again and again I've needed, I've wanted to be prepared — *better* prepared.

But that's not what the apostle Paul is speaking about here in Romans. "I am ready to preach," he says, "I'm willing to face up to the great responsibility." Paul knew that meant persecution; he knew it meant danger; he knew it meant spending energy; it meant being despised and abused. At the same time, he knew it meant the glorious thrill of heralding the good news so that those who lived in darkness might see the light, might come to know the truth as it is in Christ. And, even if perhaps he were not fully prepared academically, Paul was willing in his soul to be a witness for Christ.

Let me quickly say, however, that Paul was also prepared. He had had a personal experience with Jesus Christ. It's one thing to read about Jesus in the precious Book. It's one thing to believe about the historical Christ. It's one thing to believe that in some way he is connected with the church. But it's quite another thing to come face to face with Jesus Christ and to recognize him as an abiding friend, an eternal Savior, God's own Son, the Christians' elder brother. Paul knew Jesus as all of these, and more.

What this world needs, I'm convinced, is more feeding and explaining from this precious Book, and more sharing of what great things the Lord has done in our own personal experience. Paul was ready. He was also prepared, not only by this personal experience of Christ as Savior but by the strenuousness of life as a Christian as well. He had traveled many miles, had been inconvenienced often, had stood before both friendly and hostile crowds, had planted the gospel among those who had never known the truth. He was prepared and could say, "I'm ready. I'm ready to tell the good news." What's more, he went out with a package of which he was not ashamed. He had a message in which he believed 100 percent, and so he could say, "I am not only willing, not only prepared, but what's more, I am not ashamed of the gospel. It is the power of God to save, to lift, to energize, to enable."

Look now at Acts 21:13. Here Paul says, "I am ready not to be bound only, but also to die at Jerusalem for the name of the Lord Jesus." Let me tell you, my Christian friends, this was no idle boast on Paul's part. You remember how Peter once boasted in a quite different fashion. "Yea, Lord," said Peter, "these things shall not happen to you." He was saying, as it were, "I'm going to spearhead every attack. I'm going to be right out where the action is." But alas, just when Jesus needed him most, Peter failed the Master. Having said this, let me hasten to add that I love Peter. Let's not forget that Peter finally and fully yielded his life to God's control; he demonstrated the same kind of courage and ability to withstand attack that characterized the apostle Paul. Isn't it true that many deacons and pastors are persons who, having failed in their own strength, in time come to an experience of consecrated yieldedness and so take their places with Peter?

"I am ready. I am ready to be bound for the sake of the gospel," Paul said. "I am ready to be put to death for the sake of the gospel. I am ready to die in Jerusalem for the sake of the gospel." Why Jerusalem? Need I tell you that when you are ridiculed and humiliated and embarrassed, the hardest place to die is the place where you're known best? And Jerusalem was such a place for Paul; it was the very heart of the Jewish religion, the place where Paul might have made his greatest contribution to Judaism. "Even in Jerusalem," says Paul, "I'm willing to die. And I'm prepared to do it for Jesus' sake."

I've often asked myself, "How did Paul come to the place where he was willing and prepared to die as a martyr for Christ?" In leafing through the Acts of the

Apostles, one of the most thrilling books in the Bible, I'm reminded how Paul might have died for the cause of Christ if he had not been dropped over the wall in a basket. And in Lystra, you remember, Paul was stoned and left to die, and would indeed have died, but for the grace of God.

Corinthians also records Paul's experiences in the preparatory school of life. Cold, hungry, naked, lonely, sick, in jail and in prison, beaten, shipwrecked, without hope: he struggled again and again just to stay alive. Yet, again and again, in those very experiences, Jesus Christ became so precious and the gospel so vital, that Paul determined to give everything he possessed, the very last drop of his life's blood, if necessary, to the Savior and the proclamation of his love.

Notice now, also, 2 Timothy 4:6 where Paul says, "I am now ready to be offered, and the time of my departure is at hand." We have come to step three in our message. We have seen, first, a consecrated personality saying, "I am willing to do the will of God"; second, a consecrated Christian saying, "I am willing to give my best, even if it means death and that in Jerusalem, of all places." Now, in the third place, we find a man with no need to boast, a man who has lived out his life and wrought well for the kingdom of God, a man who went into every known area of his day and planted groups of Christian believers. Now, aged, work almost finished, in a prison with judgment upon his head and soon to die, this man in that seemingly tragic hour penned his writings to the glory of God and to the blessing of all mankind. "I am now ready to be offered." How many times had Paul said that? Often he had longed to die. He knew the truth of the gospel. He believed in heaven and eternal life. He knew the joys prepared for those who love God. Knowing those joys in a measure, he desired to depart and to be with Jesus Christ. So this readiness was nothing new. But now, in his willingness to die, Paul says, in effect, "I have finished the work which God gave me to do. I've run my race. I've run it in the consciousness of all the witnesses of all the ages. I've poured out my life — I've poured some of it into young people, as well as others, new converts in the faith who will carry on in the days ahead. I'm ready. Into thy hands, Lord Jesus, I slip mine for eternity."

Let me ask you: Are you living a life of readiness? Are you ready and willing to preach the gospel to those who do not know the Savior? Are you ready to do what Jesus wants you to do? Are you ready to suffer for his sake? Are you ready to die in the service of the Lord Christ? Are you even willing to die?

9

Be Not Deceived!

"Be not deceived; God is not mocked: for whatsoever a man soweth, that shall he also reap. For he that soweth to his flesh shall of the flesh reap corruption; but he that soweth to the Spirit shall of the Spirit reap life everlasting" (Galatians 6:7-8). Add to this passage 1 John 1:9: "If we confess our sins, he is faithful and just to forgive us our sins, and to cleanse us from all unrighteousness."

No one wants to be deceived. That's one reason why the masses trusted Billy Sunday and believed his presentation of Jesus Christ: Billy Sunday called a spade a spade. He knew the devil and detested him. He knew the meaning of sin and was desperately afraid of it. He ran to Jesus as the men and women of the Old Testament ran to the cities of refuge. You and I, too, must declare our unwillingness to continue to be deceived.

Paul's use of the word "deceived" is an interesting study. In Galatians it means, literally, "Quit wandering around. Quit acting contrary to fact. Look sin straight in the eye." Be not deceived!

It seems to me that the Holy Spirit is calling attention to three clear facts. First of all, sin is a reality. It's in me, it's in others. When Paul expressed a common feeling of woe on the part of all mankind, he said, "O wretched man that I am! who shall deliver me from the body of this death?" (Romans 7:24). That statement, moreover, would chill the heart of everyone were it not for the additional words of victory that follow: "I thank God through Jesus Christ our Lord." Sin is here. It is real and awful. Every correctional institution and gospel rescue mission testifies to this fact. It's in me, it's in you.

In the second place, Scripture testifies to this universality of sin. Every noble character mentioned in the Bible was redeemed from the bondage and the power, and finally delivered from the very presence of sin. To those who will listen the Bible declares: "All have sinned and come short of the glory of God. . . . All we like sheep have gone astray. . . ." Scripture confirms our observations and experiences.

In the third place, conscience tells us that sin is real. Despite the popularity of calling sin simply a lack of knowledge, a lack of training, something that we don't understand, and something that just happens, we must admit that sin is sin; it is enmity toward God. Every time we do wrong, we have an inner awareness of having done wrong. Conscience always challenges the wrong and wicked. Why, then, should I, should you, be deceived? Why should we be led astray? Sin is in me. Sin is in others. Sin is in our world. The Bible speaks of this fact in no uncertain terms. What's more, I have an inner witness that constantly betrays me. Do not be deceived about sin!

"God is not mocked." I looked up this word "mocked" to determine its original setting and meaning. It means literally to sneer at, or to deride. What Paul obviously wants to emphasize, then, is the folly of denying that doing wrong brings a harvest of sorrow and punishment. Since sin is present and God despises sin, and since God gave his Son as a perfect sacrifice for sin, how can we believe that a man who lives twenty, thirty, fifty, seventy years in sin will not reap sorrow and punishment for that sin? Be not deceived. No one can sneer at God. God cannot, will not, be brushed aside so that I may selfishly go my own way and do exactly as I please.

Sin brings death! It has always brought death. War reflects sin; this has been admitted down through the ages. Yet the Bible says there will be wars and rumors of wars right up to the very moment when the clouds are suddenly parted and God comes for the church in the person of his Son, Jesus Christ.

Sin, war, pestilence, famine, death — these are always related; they're a vicious chain of circumstances. Don't be deceived! Don't believe for a single moment that you can explain away all these things. Perhaps we're in the present mess because we have not taken our stand as Christian men and women. We haven't glorified God and lived for him as we should have in the world. We haven't been honest enough to identify the problem of our age as the problem that has beset every age, namely that of S-I-N. Many of us stick our heads in the sand. We wash our hands to rid ourselves of the idea. We live our lives blindly indifferent to the sin around us everywhere. Let's face it: We are responsible for many a person dying without a knowledge of Christ. Only the application of the blood of God's eternal Son can eradicate S-I-N from human nature.

Sin leads to spiritual death! Sin brings separation from

God and robs me of my right to fellowship with him, my Maker, my Savior, and my eternal Friend. While it is true that God can forgive sin and remove the guilt of sin, nevertheless the time lost, the energy wasted in that sinning cannot be restored. God will not give back the minutes nor bring back the energy lost. He will heal the hurt, yes, but the scar of sinning will always remain.

Sin does not pay. A police officer may tell you how to live to meet the requirements of the law and thus stay out of trouble. But that isn't what you need. Our schools may give information to help us to meet the responsibilities of daily living. But that isn't what we need. There's something inside us that will not let us go. That's why, taken together, these two passages of Scripture are so important and so wonderful: "Be not deceived; God is not mocked"; "If we confess our sins, he is faithful and just to forgive us our sins, and to cleanse us from all unrighteousness."

Sin, you must realize, is in the bloodstream of the human race. The things I do each day that displease God and ruin my testimony are sins. Of course, I want to get rid of my sins, but most of all I need to get rid of S-I-N. The only way known to man, past or present, to get rid of sin is by faith in Jesus Christ. To accept God's sacrifice, that blood atonement made on Calvary's cross, to see myself shorn of all I have believed myself to be, to stand in the helpless, undone condition of a sinner eternally damned, is to take my first step in the right direction. To stand before the cross and gaze on the One who knew no sin yet became sin that I, in my unrighteousness, might know the righteousness of God, and to see him on the cross in my stead, is to understand the meaning of his death for sin, for my sin. By faith in his redemption I become reconciled to God. The truth of this transaction is applied to my heart, for out of the heart proceed all the issues of life.

Something very real takes place, and, while I am not instantaneously made perfect, the bent of my natural life (which is always in the direction of wrong) is suddenly changed by the power of the Son of God who is able to break the shackles of sin and death. I now walk the pathway of true life. While I may slip, be disheartened at times, may displease God, to my sorrow, nevertheless I have assurance of spiritual cleansing and healing and health. If I look sin straight in the eye and fight, not in my own but in the Lord's strength, God will grant victory over sin.

Let me say two things in summary. First of all, there must come back to America, and to the hearts and lives of both the saved and the unsaved, a scriptural sense of sin and of its awfulness.

Sin today is as dark as it ever was. But the power of Jesus' blood to cleanse away that darkness is as great, too, as it has ever been. "What a wonderful Savior is Jesus our Lord!"

One of Gypsy Smith's favorite testimonies in song was, as I remember it:

"Wonderful, wonderful Jesus,
In the heart he implanteth a song;
A song of deliverance, of courage, of strength,
In the heart he implanteth a song."

And second, remember that you can be saved from sin and its awfulness by faith in Jesus Christ as Savior from that sin. Perhaps you have seen Holman Hunt's great picture, "The Light of the World." Someone has said this about it: "We see One with patient, gentle face, standing at a door which is ivy-covered, as if long closed. He is girt with the priestly breastplate. He bears in his hand the lamp of truth. He stands and knocks. There is no answer and he still stands and knocks. His eye tells of love; his face beams with yearning. You look closely and you perceive that there is no knob or latch on the outside of the door. It can be opened only from within.

"Do you see the meaning? The spirit of God comes to your heart's door and knocks. He stands there while storms gather and break upon his unsheltered head, while the sun declines, and night comes on with its chills and its heavy dews. He waits and knocks, but you must open the door yourself. The only latch is inside."

This Christ, my friends, offers you life and pardon and peace — accept him as your Savior. If you already know that life, that pardon, and that peace, then rejoice and make known to others the joy of this blessed experience. "Be not deceived"; ask God either to save you, for Jesus' sake, or to make you a more vigorous, productive disciple.

10

Launch Out!

In Matthew 4:21 we read: "And going on from thence, he saw other two brethren, James the son of Zebedee, and John his brother, in a ship with Zebedee their father, mending their nets; and he called them."

This verse introduces us to Zebedee and Company, commercial fishermen, a father, his two sons, and their hired help who wrested a living from the sea. Here they are, mending their nets. Nets in those days — and they haven't changed much across the years — were sometimes circular. Or they might be short dragnets or perhaps of a deep-sea variety that could be dropped twenty-five to thirty feet. Men used to dive down and pull up the weighted ends of these deep-sea nets and empty the catch into their boats. Sometimes, however, the net would not be filled with fish; then they had the disappointment of pulling in an empty net;

sometimes holes had been torn in the nets. Perhaps Zebedee and his sons were mending such nets.

Have you ever watched commercial fishermen mending nets? Hour after hour they weave heavy twine into the big and little holes. I once asked a fisherman how those holes developed. There are several explanations.

Often they are caused by great storms. The heavy pounding of the sea, the surging of billions upon billions of gallons of water tears and pulls at the nets held by giant pilings. After the storm when the men lift the nets, they hardly expect to find a big catch of fish. Instead, they expect to find gaping holes and to face the slow job of mending their nets.

Holes are often caused, too, by big fish. In John 21:11, you remember, the disciples pulled in big fish, but because Jesus was near at hand, their nets did not break. That must have been a great fishing experience. Sometimes, of course, big fish caught in a net will set up a real battle to escape and thus will tear the strings of the net.

In the third place, holes may be caused because nets are snagged by some obstacle. It could be, too, that nets tear because they are used too much, or conversely, because they are used too little.

Well, what does all this mean to us? In the first place, you remember Jesus said that every Christian is a fisherman. All of us are fishermen. "Follow me," said Jesus, "and I will make you fishers of men." Jesus is saying, "I will make you take men alive for God." That's our task. We are fishers after men. We are to go out after those who do not know Jesus Christ. We are to bring them back alive and see them dedicated to his will, consecrated to his purpose, determined to yield every ounce of personality to him. That's our task.

I don't need to tell you that there are plenty of unsaved

fish in the sea, great masses of people, particularly in our big cities, who are far from God, who have no knowledge of the salvation available in Jesus Christ. We've got to be better fishermen.

Perhaps our nets are full of holes and need to be mended. Let's pull them in and check them over. Let's mend them, mend them, mend them. Let's make them as strong as possible so they'll weather every obstacle. Then let's take our fishing instructions from Jesus. "Launch out into the deep," he tells us. Stop being satisfied with surface fishing. Launch out into the deep and determine that under God you'll bring in a real harvest of souls.

Such fishing may involve visiting our neighbors or going from door to door in our communities to win the unsaved. Or it may mean going out into places where the gospel has never been preached and giving our entire lives to fishing in those distant seas.

You remember Jesus' instructions when the disciples had caught no fish: "Let down your net on the right side of the ship." He said in this business of winning men and women for him there is a right way and a wrong way. The Master says, "Let it down on the right side." We must fish according to Jesus' instructions.

Let me tell you what, under God, I believe to be the best way to win people to Christ. Be so completely won to Christ yourself that your life will be your greatest witness and greatest sermon. Demonstrate that Christ has been able to do something good with a no-good like yourself. That's the right way. What the world needs more than ever is to see young men and young women, middle-aged men, middle-aged women, successful business people, older men and older women who live joyful, Christ-honoring lives and to hear them tell what the Lord has done for them. Such testimonies and demonstrations are contagious.

Launch out into the deep. Let the Lord direct you to the right fishing spot and show you where to drop the net. Sometimes there'll be fish that are caught only by prayer and fasting — the Lord will teach you how to do that, too. Some fish just don't want to be caught.

Actually there are many such people. They're quite satisfied to live selfish, mean, miserable, indifferent lives, or lives they think are good enough. They are determined not to be caught. There's a real price to pay to win such people, that of prayer and fasting. Are you willing to pay that price?

Never, in this business of fishing, forget what Jesus said: "Without me ye can do nothing. I am your indispensable partner. You and I are linked eternally in the task. *I* will make *YOU* fishers of men."

11

In Step with Jesus

The very last words in John 14 read: "Arise, let us go hence." A good paraphrase might be: "Get up, so we can get going." Jesus said those words as he was about to realize the most important thing in his life or in the lifetime of the whole human race. He had been talking with his friends about the kingdom of God and had shared a last meal with them. They had talked about the great plan and program of God. But now Jesus was saying, gently but firmly, "You must not remain here. The gospel is not something to be feasted upon and enjoyed all the while. You must go out into the highways and the byways. You must stand in the market place. You must live this gospel message wherever life takes you. Arise, let us go."

I'm glad Jesus said, "Let *us* go." I would be afraid to be thrust out into the world alone to live the gospel, for

I know my weaknesses. I'm only too aware that my life cannot be pleasing in his sight a single day without him. Thank God that Jesus doesn't simply say, "Go." He says, "Let *us* go": I am to walk in step with Jesus.

When we first come to Christ, he says: "Follow me." But as we grow and mature, he says: "Arise, let us go." We are to be in step with Jesus, walking side by side with him.

When I was a boy, I lived in Cumberland County and in Cape May County, New Jersey. Those were marshy areas and in the winter months my father and I used to go trapping. I had my own little hip boots. They looked like my father's, and I was proud of them. How excited I was those days we'd go out together! When we got to the danger spots in the meadows, my father would say to me, "Now, son, step just where I step." And I tried ever so hard. But eventually Dad forgot my little legs and feet and my little steps, and I wouldn't be able to keep up. I'd land in a salt pond, and my little hip boots would fill with water. Then father would turn around and say, "Why didn't you step where I *told* you to step?" He should have known I just couldn't!

Jesus is saying, "Let's walk together." And Jesus never forgets. He knows the length of my stride and he knows my strength. He knows what I can and what I can't manage. And, because he knows and because he does not forget, we walk together.

I like to go walking with people. I've never been too enthusiastic about this business of following the leader. I never really cared too much about playing the game called "The Whip," for somehow I always got to be at the tail end. But I like to walk along with someone. I don't like a companion, though, who's all the time doing a skip and a hop, somebody who evidently notices he's not in step and makes a quick little jump. Then I make a little jump and we find ourselves just hippety-hopping down the street! I don't like that.

It's a wonderful thing to step out together. It was the prophet Amos who said, "You will be always out of step with men and women unless you are in agreement." Believe me, you cannot walk with Christ unless you are in hearty agreement with all he wants you to do and be. And so, if I am to be in step, my Christian friends, if I am to walk life's highway with Jesus Christ, if my Christian life is to be really thrilling as it ought to be, I must keep in step with Christ. For too long, many of us Christians have thought we could live exactly as we pleased and then, at the close of day, ask forgiveness and think that the calendar would be wiped clean. Or we may have thought we could live the way we pleased day after day, but on Sunday come to church for a kind of purification; then start another week just the same as before. Let's mature in our Christian faith. Let's realize that if we walk with Jesus Christ, there must be a Christian manliness about us. We must have justifiable pride. We must be determined in our souls that we shall be what Christ would have us be, so that people who observe us will see that we are in step with Jesus.

You remember how there were those who always tried to find fault with Jesus. They criticized everything he did on Monday. They would have crucified him for anything he did on Sunday. They watched Jesus all the time. My friends, somebody knows you are a Christian. There are people who know you are identified with the church. And because you confess faith in Christ and because you're identified with the Christian church, there are certain people who will criticize you severely. When Jesus was accused, he turned to his critics and said, "And which of you convinceth me of sin?" We can't say that, of course, but even so, we are to live our lives so that there shall not be even the appearance of evil. We are to live openly and aboveboard as in a glass case, to be known and read of men everywhere. We are to demonstrate what God can do in a life that is redeemed by the blood of his son, Jesus. We must walk in step with Jesus.

Think of Jesus on the cross, looking down with great anguish upon the multitude. Some ridiculed, some cursed; yet Jesus said, "Father, forgive them for they know not what they do."

My friends, we must be like our Lord in how we live. We must be at peace in the midst of conflict, we must be spiritual amidst hypocrisy; we must suffer, if need be, without complaint.

We must also be in step with Christ in our work. One of the great passages in the New Testament describes Jesus like this: He went about doing good. In endless labor from early morning till late at night, he gave himself to one and all. He often said, "My father worketh hitherto, and I work." But remember Jesus said to his followers: "Greater works than these shall *you* do, because I go to my Father."

You may remember David Livingstone. The death of his wife really shook him to the very foundations of his being. Friends besought Livingstone to take things easy after her death, but no, he worked all the harder, morning, noon, and night, giving himself in ministry to the people to whom he had been called of God, until at last people said, "You, too, will burn yourself out in the heat of Africa." But David Livingstone said, "I have discovered the sweat of one's brow is not a curse. It is a tonic." So, in step with Jesus Christ, Livingstone drove a wedge for the gospel into that vast continent so that today, great companies of believers rise up and call him blessed.

We live in a needy day and generation; lip service to Christ is not enough. We must step out and must walk with Jesus so that people everywhere will know, by what we *do* as well as by what we say, that we're on fire for God.

One other thing we must remember as a Christian who gets up and steps out in step with Christ: We must do something about love. John tells us many, many times how God loves us, how he loves the whole human race, and how he gave himself that we might know eternal life.

It was said of the early Christians, "See how they love one another." And Jesus said, "By this shall all men know that you are my disciples, if ye have love one for another."

Do you love Christ? Do you love his church? Do you love the fellowship of believers, the communion of saints? We cannot walk with Jesus if we do not love as he loved. As we rub shoulders in the market place, as we walk down the avenue, his compassion must become our compassion, his sympathy our sympathy, his understanding our understanding, his love our love. God loves the unlovely. Remember he first loved us. And if Jesus Christ could so love us condemned and unclean sinners, who are we to say we are followers of Christ if we hate, are critical, and are bitter?

Let us get up and go for Christ. Let us walk in step with him, live for him, love as he loves.